Renal Diet Cookbook

The Beginner's Guide to a Low Protein, Sodium, Potassium, and Phosphorus Kidney-Friendly Diet

By: Haley Joseph

Table of Contents

Introduction

The renal diet is a way of eating that has been designed by medical professionals to suit the dietary needs of anyone who suffers from either renal failure or has kidneys that don't operate as they should.

For those with compromised kidney function, the renal diet helps you to reduce or cut out high-sodium foods, which is just one contributing factor that builds up waste in your blood. Since your diet affects your blood, the goal for anyone with compromised kidney function should be to keep it as clean as possible, which also means that you are going to have to say goodbye to refined sugars — and, yes, even alcohol.

Nonetheless, this renal diet cookbook is filled with many recipes that will keep you healthy and your kidneys operating at their optimal function, but are also satisfying. It's stressful enough having to deal with a medical condition, especially if it's chronic and you have to manage it properly for a long time or the rest of your life, without not being able to enjoy the food you want. Now, while you can't have traditional foods that you may have considered to be fit for your palate, you can take a shot at the recipes in this cookbook, where you will find some hope to relieve your cravings.

Spoiler alert: even if you have to cut down on refined sugars in your diet, you still get to have dessert — which does, in fact, include chocolate mousse and cheesecake!

Apart from food, you have to understand that to keep your blood as waste-free as possible, you must also consider the liquids you consume in your diet. As you can imagine, if you drink alcohol and have complications with your kidneys, your organs can't filter the alcohol, so you have to remove it from your diet. The same goes for drinks and foods that are high in sodium, protein, and phosphorus, all of which need to be consumed in low quantities to keep your blood waste-free.

By following the renal diet, there's no talk of curing renal failure or chronic kidney disease, but you can slow the process down significantly. How you treat your body every day, and especially what you eat, is an important factor in sustaining your health. The renal diet can also promote improved kidney function, which can help the body eliminate any toxins in the blood.

Foods to Avoid

Renal diets focus on foods low in sodium, protein, and phosphorus only. In some cases, the diet also requires you to eat a diet low in calcium and potassium, depending on how your body responds to these minerals. To rule out whether you can or can't eat calcium- or potassium-rich foods, you need to consult a renal dietitian. You will also need to consult the dietician about your diet plan to ensure that you're on the right track, which will depend on the type and severity of your condition.

Although not everyone will be recommended the same guidelines to follow with their eating plan, some substances should be monitored by anyone who has any issues with their kidneys.

Foods to avoid include:

Sodium

Found in most natural foods, sodium is a mineral that you may have mistaken thought of as salt. However, though sodium can be found in salt, which is in many foods, salt consists of sodium and chloride combined. Some foods also contain sodium in different forms than just the compound found in salt. If you've discussed nutrition with your doctor or a dietitian before, you may have been consulted to remove processed foods from your diet. This is recommended for patients with chronic kidney disease or renal failure, as processed foods contain much higher levels of sodium since salt is usually added to them.

Now, just because you should watch your sodium intake doesn't mean that you shouldn't be having any at all. The mineral makes up one of three electrolytes that are required for your body to be balanced. Sodium, chloride, and potassium control the fluids that go in and out of your body's cells and tissues.

Sodium plays a very important role in our bodies by regulating our blood volume, blood pressure, muscle contraction, and nerve function. It also keeps an acid-base balance in the blood, and controls how much fluid our body eliminates. The reason sodium intake should be monitored in kidney patients is that a patient with compromised kidney function can't eliminate excess fluid and sodium from the body, which can cause it to build up in the bloodstream and tissues. This will cause extreme thirst, high blood pressure, edema (swelling in the hands, legs, and face), heart failure by overworking the heart, and shortness of breath. Due to the potential risks of consuming too much sodium, patients need to constantly keep track of what's in their food by checking food labels; take note of their serving sizes; opt for fresh meats over packaged ones; choose fresh fruit and vegetables instead of canned, frozen, or packaged; avoid processed foods; and compare different brands to see what works best for their diet. When it comes to spices, salt shouldn't be an ingredient — don't add salt to any homemade meals, and limit sodium to 400 mg per meal or 150 mg per snack.

Potassium

When you think of potassium, your mind may gravitate to bananas, which is a real shame because who doesn't love bananas, right? But that's not entirely it. Potassium is not only present in bananas, and just because kidney patients have to watch their intake of potassium, just like with sodium, it doesn't mean that the body doesn't still need it. As one of the three electrolytes in the body, potassium plays an important role in maintaining fluids and the electrolyte balance in our bloodstream. Since it's the kidneys' responsibility to maintain the correct amount of potassium in the body by expelling any excess amounts into the urine, with compromised kidney function, your body won't be able to get rid of it effectively.

With an inability to remove excess potassium from the body, the mineral can build up and cause a slow pulse, irregular heartbeat, muscle weakness, heart attacks, and even be fatal. So, if you're a kidney patient, you must take nutrition very seriously. It's something that you can't ignore, as it could be harmful to your health. To monitor your potassium intake, talk with your renal dietitian about developing an eating plan. You can also consult a professional about the meals in this cookbook and see whether it's a fit for your particular condition. Furthermore, you should limit foods that are rich in potassium, limit all dairy and milk products to only 8 ounces per day, bulk up on fresh fruits and vegetables in your diet, avoid salt substitutes or seasonings that contain potassium, read labels to avoid the ingredient potassium chloride, monitor serving size, and keep a daily food journal to track everything you're eating each day.

Phosphorus

As another important mineral in the body, phosphorus is crucial for bone development and maintenance. It assists with developing organs and connective tissues, and supports muscle movement, which means that it is very important. When we eat phosphorus-rich foods, our small intestines are responsible for absorbing the mineral to store it in our bones. Our kidneys are responsible for removing the mineral from the blood, but when kidney function is compromised, the organs take longer to remove any excess. As a result, calcium can be pulled from the bones, weakening them, which could lead to harmful calcium deposits in the lungs, blood vessels, heart, and eyes.

Phosphorus-rich foods include fast food, meat, cheese, milk, carbonated beverages, canned fish, and seeds. To keep phosphorus levels in check, foods that are low in phosphorus should be consumed, serving size should be controlled, and a diet must consist of mainly fresh food. Packaged foods should be avoided.

Protein

Although protein isn't such a big problem for maintaining healthy kidneys, when protein is ingested, waste products are created, which gets filtered by the kidneys' nephrons. With added renal proteins, waste is then turned into urine. Damaged kidneys, however, cannot remove protein as waste, causing it to accumulate in the blood. That's why it's necessary to pay attention to the type of protein you are eating. For Chronic Kidney Disease (CKD), the recommended daily intake of protein will differ.

Since protein is important for the maintenance of tissues and for fulfilling bodily roles, it should still be added to a kidney patient's diet, but only through high-quality sources like turkey, lean beef, chicken, eggs, cottage cheese, fish (fresh and not canned), Greek yogurt, protein smoothies, nutrition drinks, and meat substitutes.

Fluids

The intake of fluid is probably one of the most important things that needs to be monitored during the later stages of CKD because normal fluid consumption causes the build-up of fluid in the body. This can become dangerous, especially for people who are on dialysis and may have a decreased urine output. With the presence of more fluid in the body, unnecessary pressure can be placed on the heart and lungs. With dialysis patients, fluid allowance is calculated regularly and requires following a dietician's fluid intake guidelines. To control the intake of fluids, don't drink more than what your doctor recommends, counting in all of the foods that you consume that could melt at room temperature, and be aware of the fluids that you cook with.

Why Is It Important to Follow a Diet Plan?

With compromised kidney function, it is crucial to stay as healthy as you can at all times, which can be done by following the diet fit for your condition. This can improve your kidney function, as well as your quality of life. By eating a balanced diet that is low in fats and salt, you can maintain a healthy weight and balanced blood pressure. If you have any other chronic conditions, like diabetes, you can also control blood sugar levels by following the renal diet. By controlling diabetes, you can prevent your kidney functioning from worsening.

The kidney-friendly diet can help prevent a build-up of minerals in the body, and help you keep track of your intake of calories, protein, fat, and carbohydrates.

Chapter 1: Breakfast

Turkey Burritos

For a deliciously satisfying and quick high-quality protein-packed breakfast option, this lean meat burrito is just the right meal for you.

Time: 10 minutes

Serving Size: 4

Prep Time: 2 minutes

Cook Time: 8 minutes

Nutritional Info:

Calories: 407

Carbs: 23 g

Fat: 24 g

Protein: 25 g

Sodium: 513 g

Potassium: 285 mg

Phosphorus: 359 mg

Ingredients:

- 4 6-inch flour burrito shells
- ½ oz of ground turkey
- 4 eggs
- ½ cup of mozzarella cheese
- ⅛ cup of olive oil
- ⅛ cup of bell peppers (red, green, and yellow — diced)
- ⅛ cup of onions (diced)
- 1 tbsp of scallions (chopped)
- 1 tbsp of cilantro (chopped)
- 1 tbsp of jalapeño peppers (diced)
- ¼ tsp of chili powder
- ¼ tsp of smoked paprika

Directions:

1. Crack the eggs into a bowl and whisk them until well combined.

2. Preheat the stove to medium heat and place a medium sauté pan on the stovetop to cook the scrambled eggs until they are cooked through and fluffy. Place the scrambled eggs into a bowl.

3. Place a large pan on the stove over medium heat and add half of the oil, turkey, onions, scallions, peppers, and cilantro to the pan. Stir all of the ingredients well. Once everything is cooked, add the remaining oil and scrambled eggs to the mixture.

4. Place the burrito shells on plates and divide the turkey and vegetable scramble mixture evenly between them. Before closing the burrito shells, top each with some grated cheese.

5. Fold the burrito shells into a wrap and serve immediately.

Food-prep tip: If you have any leftovers, you can seal them in an airtight glass container and place them in the fridge for up to two days.

Blueberry Muffins

Who said you couldn't have a sweet option for breakfast? These muffins are perfect for meal prepping if you increase the quantity of the ingredients, and are approved for CKD non-dialysis, dialysis, diabetes, renal condition preferences (low-protein), and poor heart health patients.

Time: 30 minutes

Serving Size: 12

Prep Time: 5 minutes

Cook Time: 25 minutes

Nutritional Info:

Calories: 170 g

Carbs: 28 g

Fat: 5 g

Protein: 3 g

Sodium: 95 mg

Potassium: 39 mg

Phosphorus: 53 mg

Ingredients:

- 1 egg
- 2 cups of flour
- 1 cup of rice milk
- 1 cup of blueberries (frozen)

- ½ cup of granulated sugar

- ¼ cup of vegetable oil

- 1 tbsp of lemon zest

- 2 tsp of baking powder

Directions:

1. Preheat the oven to 375°F.

2. Combine the flour, sugar, and baking powder in a medium mixing bowl.

3. In a separate small bowl, whisk together the egg, vegetable oil, lemon zest, and rice milk.

4. Pour the mixed liquid ingredients into the flour mixture, and mix them lightly until moistened, but do not overmix.

5. Fold the blueberries gradually and gently into the batter.

6. Add paper cups to a muffin tin and spoon the batter into the cups.

7. Bake the muffins for 25 minutes or until cooked through.

Food-prep tip: Prep the muffins ahead of time as an easy on-the-go breakfast option.

Berry Flax Smoothie

If you're looking for a liquid option to start your day, you can break the sleep fast with this smoothie, which is filled with all of the antioxidants, cleansing qualities, and healthy fats you need to get a good start to your day.

Time: 5 minutes

Serving Size: 1

Prep Time: 5 minutes

Cook Time: 0 minutes

Nutritional Info:

Calories: 107

Carbs: 17.8 g

Fat: 3 g

Protein: 1.6 g

Sodium: 28.1 mg

Potassium: 29.7 mg

Phosphorus: 21.2 mg

Ingredients:

- 1 cup of rice milk
- ¼ cup of mixed berries (frozen)
- ¼ cup of cucumber
- 1 tbsp of ground flaxseed
- 1 tsp of honey

- 1 fresh mint leaf

Directions:

1. Prepare all of the smoothie ingredients by pureeing the blueberries and chopping up the cucumber and mint leaf.

2. Add all of the ingredients to the blender and blend them at a medium to high speed. For the desired consistency, add more rice milk.

3. Serve cold.

Food-prep tip: Blend the berry smoothie the night before and add it to a sealed canning jar or glass bottle for an easy, on-the-go breakfast option.

Cheesesteak Quiche

This cheesy quiche may not seem like the healthiest of breakfasts, but it's approved for the renal diet to support a variety of kidney conditions. This delicious option is not only great for breakfast but also any other time of the day, which means it can be stored for lunch or dinner, too. If you're a pastry-lover, this one's for you!

Time: 50 minutes

Serving Size: 6

Prep Time: 10 minutes

Cook Time: 40 minutes

Nutritional Info:

Calories: 527

Carbs: 22g

Fat: 19 g

Protein: 22 g

Sodium: 392 mg

Potassium: 308 mg

Phosphorus: 281 mg

Ingredients:

- ½ oz of sirloin steak meat (shaved and chopped)
- 1" x 9" prepared pie crust
- 5 eggs

- 1 cup of cream

- 1 cup of onions (diced)

- ½ cup of cheddar cheese (shredded)

- 2 tbsp of canola oil

- ½ tsp of ground black pepper

Directions:

1. Prepare the sirloin steak by chopping it into coarse pieces.

2. Sauté the chopped steak with the onions in a medium pan with oil, until the meat is brown and cooked through. Set aside to cool for 10 minutes, and then add grated cheese.

3. In a large bowl, beat together the cream and eggs with black pepper until properly mixed.

4. Spread the cheese and steak mix onto the bottom of the par-cooked pie-crust.

5. Pour the egg mixture over the top part of the crust, and then bake it for 30 minutes at 350°F.

6. Cover the quiche with foil, then turn off the oven and allow it to sit for 10 minutes before serving it hot.

Food-prep tip: Store the cheesesteak quiche in an airtight container in the fridge for up to three days.

Banana Pancakes

These banana pancakes are low in sodium, making them a healthy and fit choice for anyone with a sweet tooth that may feel like they've been restricted from sugar for too long. This recipe makes 4 servings, which can be shared among friends or family for a healthy, but delicious breakfast option.

Time: 35 minutes

Serving Size: 3 pancakes (serves 4)

Prep Time: 5 minutes

Cook Time: 30 minutes

Nutritional Info:

Calories: 288

Carbs: 45 g

Fat: 9 g

Protein: 9 g

Sodium: 453 mg

Potassium: 205.4 g

Phosphorus: 181 mg

Ingredients:

- 1 banana (mashed)
- 1 egg
- 1 cup of water (boiling)
- 1 cup of blueberries (to top)
- ½ cup of rolled oats
- ½ cup of whole wheat flour
- ½ cup of all-purpose flour
- ½ cup of skim milk
- ¼ cup of plain yogurt (fat-free)
- 2 tbsp of canola oil
- 2 tbsp of brown sugar
- 1 ½ tsp of baking powder
- ¼ tsp of baking soda
- ¼ tsp of salt
- ¼ tsp of cinnamon

Directions:

1. Add and combine the oats and hot water in a large bowl, then allow it to sit for 2 minutes until the oats are creamy.

2. Stir brown sugar and canola oil into the oat mixture and set aside to cool slightly.

3. Add the all-purpose flour, whole-wheat flour, baking soda, baking powder, salt, and cinnamon to a separate medium bowl, and whisk the ingredients together to blend.

4. To the oat mixture, add the mashed banana, milk, and yogurt. Stir well until everything is blended.

5. Beat the egg in a separate small bowl, then add it and the flour mixture to the oat mixture. Stir the ingredients together once more until everything is blended.

6. Place a large non-stick frying pan over medium heat. Once it is heated, spoon ¼ cup of the batter into the center of the pan and cook it for at least 2 minutes, or until the top of the pancake's surface is covered in bubbles, with the edges lightly browned. Flip the pancake over and cook it on the other side for 2 to 3 minutes. Repeat this step with the remaining pancake batter.

7. Serve three pancakes per serving, topped with blueberries and a drizzle of honey.

Food-prep tip: Place the pancakes in an airtight container in the refrigerator, and serve them, three pancakes per serving, slightly heated.

Tofu Scramble

For a savory and filling breakfast, this is a tasty alternative to eggs, which you will find is a breakfast staple for a healthy diet. If you're looking for something different, the tofu scramble alternative is perfect for you.

Time: 25 minutes

Serving Size: 2

Prep Time: 5 minutes

Cook Time: 20 minutes

Nutritional Info:

Calories: 213

Carbs: 10 g

Fat: 13 mg

Protein: 18 g

Sodium: 24 mg

Potassium: 467 mg

Phosphorus: 242 mg

Ingredients:

- 1 cup of firm tofu (chopped)
- ½ cup of red and green bell peppers (diced)
- 1 tsp of garlic powder (no added salt)
- 1 tsp of onion powder (no added salt)
- 1 tsp of olive oil

- 1 garlic clove (minced)

Directions:

1. Over medium-high heat, add olive oil to a medium-sized non-stick pan.

2. Add the garlic and peppers to the pan and sauté them for 1 to 2 minutes.

3. Add the tofu, garlic, garlic, and onion powder and stir the ingredients to combine. Cook for 15 to 20 minutes, or until the mixture is golden brown. When water starts evaporating from the mixture, remove the pan from the stove.

4. Divide the tofu scramble into two servings and serve hot.

Food-prep tip: Store leftovers in an airtight container for the next day.

French Toast

If you're a fan of apple pie, this dish will come close to what your taste buds are looking for, minus the guilt. This is a low-protein breakfast option fit for CKD patients, or anyone living with kidney health issues.

Time: 4 hours and 55 minutes

Serving Size: 9

Prep Time: 5 minutes

Cook Time: 50 minutes + 4 hours (to refrigerate)

Nutritional Info:

Calories: 432

Carbs: 63 g

Fat: 16 g

Protein: 9 g

Sodium: 380 mg

Potassium: 210 mg

Phosphorus: 136 mg

Ingredients:

- 6 eggs
- 3 apples
- 1 pound Italian bread (loaf)
- 1 ½ cup of rice milk
- ¾ cup of brown sugar
- ½ cup of cranberries

28

- ½ cup of butter (unsalted)

- 1 tbsp of vanilla

- 3 tsp of cinnamon

Directions:

1. Peel, core, and slice the apples into thin slices.

2. Prep a 13" x 9" baking dish. Melt the butter and combine it with brown sugar and cinnamon, then add the apples and cranberries. Mix the ingredients until all the fruit is well coated.

3. Spread the apple mixture over the bottom of the baking dish.

4. Cut the loaf of bread into ¾" slices and place them on top of the apples in the baking dish.

5. In a bowl, mix together the eggs, vanilla, rice milk, and 2 tsp of cinnamon until well combined. Pour the wet mixture over the bread, covering the entire baking dish. Cover the dish and refrigerate it for at least 4 hours or leave it in the refrigerator overnight.

6. Preheat the oven to 375°F, cover the dish with foil, and bake the french toast for 30 minutes.

7. Once done, remove the foil and bake for another 15 minutes. The result should be slightly golden brown.

8. Remove the dish from the oven and allow it to stand for at least 5 minutes before you cut it into 9 servings.

9. Serve the french toast warm, topped with a drizzle of honey.

Food-prep tip: Store the remaining servings of French toast in the refrigerator by covering the baking dish with tin foil. It will keep for up to 2 days.

Apple Maple Granola

For a sweet, low-protein option with only 3 mg of sodium, granola is perfect for a kidney-friendly breakfast or served as a daily snack. If you're short on time, prep this delicious apple granola dish over the weekend — it will last as a tasty breakfast or snack option all week long.

Time: 50 minutes

Serving Size: 16 (½ cup per serving)

Prep Time: 0 minutes

Cook Time: 50 minutes

Nutritional Info:

Calories: 162

Carbs: 25 g

Fat: 6 g

Protein: 2 g

Sodium: 3 mg

Potassium: 107 mg

Phosphorus: 70 mg

Ingredients:

- 3 cups of rolled oats
- 3 cups of puffed rice cereal
- 3.4 oz of apple chips (packaged, baked)
- ½ cup of dried cranberries
- ½ cup of applesauce (unsweetened)
- 1/4cup of coconut oil (melted)
- ¼ cup of maple syrup (100% pure)
- 1 tsp of vanilla extract
- 1 tsp of cinnamon

Directions:

1. Preheat the oven to 275°F and prepare a baking dish by lining it with sheets of parchment paper.

2. Combine the rolled oats, puffed cereal, cinnamon, dried cranberries, and apple chips in a large bowl.

3. In a small bowl, combine the applesauce, coconut oil, vanilla extract, and maple syrup. Once done, mix the wet mixture with the dry ingredients until well combined.

4. Divide the mixture between 2 medium- to large-sized baking sheets.

5. Bake the granola for 50 minutes to an hour, changing the pan's position once you reach the halfway point. You can place one pan on the top rack and one on the bottom, and change the position of each after 25 minutes.

6. Serve the granola with a serving of Greek yogurt or a dairy-free milk alternative, like rice milk or almond milk.

Food-prep tip: Store the granola in canning jars or airtight containers for up to 7 days in a cool, dry place.

Veggie Omelet

This omelet is low in calories but high in essential nutrients, which means it's a great meal option for weight loss. While it provides you with a good source of protein, you won't overdo your protein intake with this meal. Another bonus is that it only takes 10 minutes to make!

Time: 10 minutes

Serving Size: 2

Prep Time: 2 minutes

Cook Time: 8 minutes

Nutritional Info:

Calories: 199

Carbs: 4 g

Fat: 15 g

Protein: 11 g

Sodium: 276 mg

Potassium: 228 mg

Phosphorus: 167 mg

Ingredients:

- 3 eggs
- ½ cup of raw button mushrooms (rinsed and sliced)
- ¼ cup of sweet red peppers (washed and diced)

34

- 2 tbsp of whipped cream cheese

- 2 tbsp of onion (diced)

- 2 tsp of butter

- 1 tsp of Worcestershire sauce

- ¼ tsp of black pepper

Directions:

1. Toss the diced mushrooms and onions together.

2. Melt 1 tsp of butter in a medium non-stick pan over medium heat.

3. Add the vegetable mix to the pan and sauté it for 5 minutes until the veggies are tender. Add the red pepper to sauté for another minute before removing the vegetables from the pan.

4. Once removed, add another tsp of butter to the pan.

5. Beat the eggs with the Worcestershire sauce until well combined. Cook the eggs over medium heat until the omelet mixture is solid and not wet. Gently start to lift the omelet on the edges to ensure all of the mixture is partially cooked.

6. Add the vegetable mixture to one half of the omelet. Follow this with a dollop of whipped cream cheese over the vegetables, and continue to cook the omelet until it is set.

7. Remove the pan from the stove and fold the omelet in half. Add the black pepper to the final product, divide the omelet into two portions, and serve hot.

Food-prep tip: Store the remaining half of the omelet in an airtight glass container in the refrigerator for up to one day.

Blueberry Cobbler

This cobbler dish is a good alternative to your daily plain bowl of oatmeal. It's filling and vegan-friendly, and can be enjoyed as a sweet option for breakfast that you will love from the moment you try it.

Time: 50 minutes

Serving Size: 8

Prep Time: 10 minutes

Cook Time: 40 minutes

Nutritional Info:

Calories: 321

Carbs: 30.4 g

Fat: 17 g

Protein: 4.8 g

Sodium: 61.2

Potassium: 188 mg

Phosphorus: 121 mg

Ingredients:

Blueberry base:

- 4 cups of blueberries (fresh or frozen)
- 2 tbsp of honey
- 1 tbsp of arrowroot powder (cornstarch)
- 1 tsp of lemon juice
- 1 tsp of vanilla extract

Cobbler:

- 1 cup of rolled oats
- 1 cup of almond flour
- 1 cup of walnuts (finely chopped)
- 1/ cup of honey
- ⅓ cup of coconut oil (melted)
- 1 tsp of vanilla extract
- ¼ tsp of Himalayan salt

Directions:

1. Preheat the oven to 350°F.

2. Mix together the blueberries, lemon juice, honey, and vanilla in a large bowl.

3. Once combined, add the arrowroot starch to the blueberry mixture and spoon the mixture into an 8" x 8" baking dish, leaving the juice in the bowl.

4. Mix the dry ingredients, including the oats, almond flour, walnuts, and salt, in a separate medium bowl.

5. Stir in the coconut oil, honey, and vanilla until everything is well combined.

6. Spread the cobbler topping evenly over the blueberries.

7. Place the baking dish in the oven to bake for 45 minutes. The topping of the dish should be golden brown once done.

8. Allow the dish to cool for 15 minutes before serving it.

Food-prep tip: Store the leftovers in the refrigerator by covering the dish with foil to seal it. It will keep for up to 4 days.

Chapter 2: Lunch

Mexican Tacos

If you are looking for a spicy and comforting lunch option for both you and your family or friends, then these Mexican tacos are just what you need. The recipe makes 7 servings, which means you can store them for up to 3 days in the refrigerator for the week, or enjoy them among a group of people.

Time: 30 minutes

Serving Size: 7 (2 tacos each)

Prep Time: 20 minutes

Cook Time: 10 minutes

Nutritional Info:

Calories: 340

Carbs: 32 g

Fat: 15 g

Protein: 19 g

Sodium: 494 mg

Potassium: 422 mg

Phosphorus: 276 mg

Ingredients:

- 14 6-inch flour tortillas
- 1 oz ground beef
- 2 cups of lettuce
- ½ cup of tomato sauce (low-sodium)
- 5 tbsp of onions
- 5 tbsp of sour cream
- 5 tbsp of mozzarella cheese
- 1 tbsp of olive oil
- Mexican seasoning: 3 tsp chili powder, 2 tsp paprika, 2 tsp ground cumin, 1 tsp onion powder, ½ tsp of garlic powder, and ⅛ tsp of black pepper.

Directions:

1. Prepare the Mexican seasoning recipe by combining the paprika, ground cumin, onion powder, garlic powder, chili powder, and black pepper.

2. Chop the lettuce and onion into small pieces.

3. On a medium non-stick pan, add 1 tbsp of olive oil and cook the ground beef for a few

minutes until it is golden brown. Once done, add the seasoning mixture and the tomato sauce.

4. Place the tortillas in the microwave oven and heat for 20 seconds until they are slightly warm.

5. Assemble the soft tacos by dividing the ground beef mixture evenly between all 14 of the tortillas.

6. Add 1 tsp of mozzarella cheese, 1 tsp of onion, 1 tsp of sour cream, and lettuce to each taco. Serve the tacos warm.

Food-prep tip: Store the tacos in airtight containers and place them in the refrigerator for up to 3 days.

Strawberry Sandwich

Who doesn't like a good sandwich — and who knew you could make the perfect one with strawberries? This is a very low-protein and low-calorie lunch option that can be enjoyed on the go. It is quick to make and easy to pack, and low in potassium and phosphorus to support any kidney condition, including dialysis.

Time: 5 minutes

Serving Size: 1

Prep Time: 5 minutes

Cook Time: 0 minutes

Nutritional Info:

Calories: 123

Carbs: 18.5 g

Fat: 3.7 g

Protein: 4 g

Sodium: 200.8 mg

Potassium: 75.2 mg

Phosphorus: 44.2 mg

Ingredients:

- 2 slices of whole-wheat sandwich bread
- 2 medium strawberries (sliced)
- 1 tbsp of cream cheese (reduced-fat)
- ¼ tsp of honey
- ⅛ tsp of orange zest (freshly grated)

Directions:

1. Combine the cream cheese, orange zest, and honey in a small bowl.

2. Plate the two slices of bread and spread them with the cheese mixture.

3. Add the strawberry slices on top of one bread slice, and close it with the other to make a sandwich.

Food-prep tip: Prep your strawberry sandwich for the next day's lunch the night before. Seal it in a Ziploc bag or an airtight plastic container in the refrigerator.

Crunch Chicken Wraps

For a high-quality protein option and a source of healthy fats, this burrito is filling and meets all your health requirements, no matter the kidney condition you may be struggling with. It also is low in carbs and calories.

Time: 10 minutes

Serving Size: 4

Prep Time: 5 minutes

Cook Time: 5 minutes

Nutritional Info:

Calories: 315

Carbs: 15 g

Fat: 21.4 g

Protein: 17.2 g

Sodium: 107.9 mg

Potassium: 480 mg

Phosphorus: 385 mg

Ingredients:
- 4 large tortillas
- 1 avocado
- 2 cups of cooked chicken breasts (shredded)
- ½ cup of mozzarella cheese
- 2 tbsp of cilantro (chopped)
- 1 tbsp of olive oil

Directions:

1. Prep a batch of chicken breasts cooked for 40 minutes at 180°F, then shred and store in the refrigerator in an airtight container.

2. Add the shredded chicken, diced avocado, cilantro, and mozzarella cheese to a medium bowl.

3. Place the tortillas flat on 4 separate plates, and add a ¼ of the chicken filling mixture.

4. Hand-roll each burrito.

5. Warm 1 tbsp of olive oil in a large non-stick pan over medium heat and add the burritos. Flip the burritos, cooking them for 1 minute on each side or until they are golden brown. Serve them warm.

Food-prep tip: Store the burritos for the week in an airtight container to enjoy as a lunch option on the go or at home. To save time, prep the chicken over the weekend to last you for meals for the week ahead.

Chicken and Broccoli Stromboli

This pizza-dough bread dish is like a hug on a cold winter's day. It's packed with nutrients and a high-quality source of protein that is also low in fat.

Time: 35 minutes

Serving Size: 4

Prep Time: 15 minutes

Cook Time: 20 minutes

Nutritional Info:

Calories: 522

Carbs: 52 g

Fat: 5 g

Protein: 38 g

Sodium: 607 mg

Potassium: 546 mg

Phosphorus: 400 mg

Ingredients:

- 1 oz of pizza dough (store-bought)
- 2 cups of cooked chicken breast (diced)
- 2 cups of broccoli florets (fresh and blanched)
- 1 cup of cheddar cheese (shredded)
- 2 tbsp of olive oil
- 1 tbsp oregano (chopped)

- 1 tbsp of garlic (chopped)

- 1 tbsp of flour

- 1 tsp of red pepper flakes (crushed)

Directions:

1. Preheat the oven to 400°F.

2. Mix the chicken, broccoli, garlic, pepper flakes, and oregano in a bowl, and set aside.

3. Dust a clean, flat tabletop surface with flour. Roll out the dough until it has reached a rectangular shape of 11" x 14".

4. Add the chicken mixture 2 inches from the dough's edge on the longer side. Roll and pinch the dough's ends, seaming it until it is tightly sealed. This can be done with a fork or the back of a coffee mug.

5. Brush the top of the dough with olive oil. Follow this by making 3 small slits at the top part of the dough.

6. Bake the dish on a lightly oiled baking tray for 10 to 12 minutes, or until it is golden brown.

7. Remove the stromboli from the oven and let it sit for 5 minutes before serving it hot.

Food-prep tip: Store the remaining stromboli in an airtight container, or cover the baking dish to seal with tin foil. It will keep in the refrigerator for up to 3 days.

Shrimp Quesadilla

This shrimp dish is filled with quality ingredients and makes a fit source of protein for anyone with a kidney condition or diabetes. It is low in carbs, low in protein, and will keep you full and satisfied until dinner.

Time: 20 minutes

Serving Size: 2

Prep Time: 10 minutes

Cook Time: 10 minutes

Nutritional Info:

Calories: 318

Carbs: 26 g

Fat: 15 g

Protein: 20 g

Sodium: 398 mg

Potassium: 276 mg

Phosphorus: 243 mg

Ingredients:

- 5 oz of shrimp (raw)
- 2 flour tortillas
- 2 tbsp of cilantro
- 2 tbsp of cheddar cheese (shredded)
- 2 tbsp of sour cream

- 1 tbsp lemon juice
- 4 tsp of salsa
- ¼ tsp of cumin
- ⅛ tsp of cayenne pepper

Directions:

1. Shell and devein the shrimp, followed by rinsing and cutting it into bite-sized pieces.

2. Chop the cilantro finely and combine it with lemon juice, cayenne pepper, and cumin in a Ziploc bag to make a marinade. Place the shrimp pieces in the bag, and allow it to sit for 5 minutes.

3. Heat a medium non-stick skillet over medium heat and add the shrimp with the remaining marinade to the skillet. Stir-fry the contents for 2 minutes, or until the shrimp turns orange. Once done, remove the skillet from the heat. Spoon the shrimp out of the marinade into a separate bowl.

4. Add sour cream to your marinade in a skillet, and then stir to mix it.

5. Heat the tortillas in the microwave for 30 seconds to a minute.

6. Spread 2 tsp of salsa onto each of the tortillas before topping it with ½ of the seasoned shrimp.

7. Sprinkle each tortilla with 1 tbsp of cheese, and spoon the sour cream mixture onto the shrimp.

8. Fold the tortilla in half to close and place it on a new skillet for a few seconds. Turn the tortilla over when it becomes slightly golden brown. Repeat this step with the other tortilla, as well.

9. Cut the tortillas into 4 pieces each, and garnish with a little cilantro and a lemon wedge to serve.

Food-prep tip: Store the tortillas in airtight sealed glass containers in the refrigerator for up to 2 days.

BBQ Chicken Pita

Who doesn't love a BBQ chicken combo for a meal? Even with CKD, dialysis, general poor kidney function, or diabetes, you can enjoy this pizza alternative, which is low in calories, fat, and offers a high-quality source of protein.

Time: 15 minutes

Serving Size: 2

Prep Time: 3 minutes

Cook Time: 12 minutes

Nutritional Info:

Calories: 320

Carbs: 37 g

Fat: 9 g

Protein: 23 g

Sodium: 523 mg

Potassium: 255 mg

Phosphorus: 221 mg

Ingredients:

- 2 6" pita bread
- 4 oz of chicken (cooked, cubed)
- ¼ cup of purple onion (sliced)
- 3 tbsp of barbecue sauce (low-sodium)
- 2 tbsp of feta cheese
- ⅛ tsp of garlic powder

Directions:

1. Preheat the oven to 350°F.

2. Prepare a baking sheet by spraying it with a layer of non-stick cooking spray.

3. Place 2 pitas on the sheet, followed by 1 ½ tbsp of barbecue sauce on each of the pitas.

4. Top with onion slices and cubed chicken, then sprinkle feta and garlic powder over the pitas.

5. Bake the pitas in the oven for 12 minutes before removing them and allowing them to cool down slightly before serving.

Food-prep tip: Slice the pitas into smaller pieces, and store them in a sealed, airtight glass container in the refrigerator for up to 3 days.

Mediterranean Bean Salad

As a light, and quick-to-make lunch, this bean salad is a step outside of the box from your traditional bowl of greens. It has a combination of delicious flavors and will leave you feeling fresh and satisfied. The salad can be served on its own as a main dish, or as a side to a good source of protein like chicken or fish. The meal is low in protein and calories.

Time: 20 minutes

Serving Size: 8

Prep Time: 20 minutes

Cook Time: 0 minutes

Nutritional Info:

Calories: 308

Carbs: 35 g

Fat: 15 g

Protein: 13 g

Sodium: 924 mg

Potassium: 500 mg

Phosphorus: 323 mg

Ingredients:

- 1 can of cannellini beans (19 oz, drained and rinsed)
- 1 can of kidney beans (19 oz, drained and rinsed)
- 1 can of chickpeas (15 oz, drained and rinsed)
- 1/2 of an English cucumber (quartered and sliced)
- 1 red bell pepper (diced)
- 1 cup of rosa tomatoes (sliced)
- ¾ cup of feta cheese (crumbled)
- ½ cup of olives (sliced)
- ½ cup of red onion (diced)
- ½ cup of fresh parsley (chopped)
- 2 tbsp of fresh basil (chopped)
- Dressing: ⅓ cup of olive oil, 2 cloves of garlic, 3 tbsp of lemon juice (freshly squeezed), 3 tbsp of red wine vinegar, 2 tsp of dijon mustard, ½ tsp of oregano, ½ tsp of sea salt, and a pinch of black pepper.

Directions:

1. Mix the dressing ingredients, including the olive oil, garlic, lemon juice, red wine vinegar, dijon mustard, oregano, sea salt, and black pepper, in a medium bowl.

2. Combine the beans, tomato, bell pepper, cucumber, olives, red onion, basil, and parsley in a large bowl.

3. Once done, pour the salad dressing over the bean salad and toss all the ingredients until everything is well coated. Add the feta once done.

4. Cover the salad and allow it to rest to get the best flavor. Alternatively, it can be served right away.

Food-prep tip: Store the salad in an airtight glass container in the refrigerator for up to 3 days.

Sloppy Joe Turkey Burger

This burger is guilt-free, offers a good source of protein, and is low in potassium and phosphorus to provide you with a kidney-friendly meal option that is packed with nutrients and tastes more like a treat than a healthy meal! So, if you're feeling any cravings coming on, this is just the traditional burger alternative for you.

Time: 25 minutes

Serving Size: 6

Prep Time: 10 minutes

Cook Time: 15 minutes

Nutritional Info:

Calories: 290

Carbs: 28 g

Fat: 9 g

Protein: 24 g

Sodium: 288 mg

Potassium: 513 mg

Phosphorus: 237 mg

Ingredients:

- 6 hamburger buns
- 1 cup of tomato sauce (low-sodium)
- ½ cup of red onion (diced)
- ½ cup of yellow bell pepper (diced)

- 1 ½ oz of ground turkey (only 7% fat)

- 2 tbsp of brown sugar

- 1 tbsp of chicken seasoning

- 1 tbsp of Worcestershire sauce

Directions:

1. In a large non-stick pan over medium heat, cook the ground turkey until it is cooked through. Do not drain the pan once cooked.

2. Add the chicken seasoning, tomato sauce, Worcestershire sauce, and brown sugar to a small bowl, and mix the ingredients until well combined.

3. Add the seasonings to the mixture, followed by the diced vegetables.

4. Reduce the heat for the turkey dish to simmer, and continue to cook it for 10 minutes.

5. Divide the turkey mixture into 6 equal portions.

6. Spread 1 tbsp of cream cheese on both sides of the hamburger bun and add a portion of turkey mixture on top of each.

Food-prep tip: Store the leftover hamburgers in a sealed, airtight container in the refrigerator for up to 3 days.

Herb-Roasted Chicken With Vegetables

For a low-protein and weight-loss diet-friendly option, this roasted dish is the go-to lunch for you.

Time: 55 minutes

Serving Size: 4

Prep Time: 10 minutes

Cook Time: 45 minutes

Nutritional Info:

Calories: 215

Carbs: 8 g

Fat: 7 g

Protein: 30 g

Sodium: 107 mg

Potassium: 580 mg

Phosphorus: 250 mg

Ingredients:

- 8 garlic cloves (minced)
- 4 chicken breasts
- 2 medium zucchini (sliced ¼-inch thick)
- 1 medium carrot (sliced ¼-inch thick)
- ½ of yellow bell pepper (sliced ¼-inch thick)
- ½ of red onion (cut into ½-inch wedges)
- 1 tbsp of olive oil

- 1 tbsp dried cilantro

- ¼ tsp of pepper

Directions:

1. Preheat the oven to 375°F.

2. Add the zucchini, bell pepper, carrot, onion, and garlic in a roasting pan and drizzle the olive oil on top.

3. Season the vegetable mixture with black pepper and mix it with a spatula to coat. Roast the vegetables for about 10 minutes.

4. In the meantime, remove the skin from the chicken, and rub the meat with black pepper and cilantro. Place the skin back on and season with added pepper and rosemary as per your preference.

5. Remove the roasting dish from the oven and place the chicken breasts onto the vegetables. Place it back in the oven to continue roasting for 35 minutes.

6. Once done, remove the dish from the oven to cool down a little before serving it.

Food-prep tip: Place the leftovers in an airtight container and keep it refrigerated for lunch for the entire week. Store it for up to 4 days.

Seafood Noodle Salad

For a quick and easy Asian-inspired meal, this noodle salad recipe is packed with high-quality protein, but in a low quantity.

Time: 20 minutes

Serving Size: 10

Prep Time: 20 minutes

Cook Time: 0 minutes

Nutritional Info:

Calories: 254

Carbs: 27 g

Fat: 11 g

Protein: 13 g

Sodium: 433 mg

Potassium: 325 mg

Phosphorus: 229 mg

Ingredients:

- 1 oz of dry spaghetti (cooked and chilled, not rinsed)
- 4 cups of cocktail shrimp (peeled, deveined, tailless, and cooked)
- 2 cups of fresh broccoli florets
- 2 cups of button mushrooms (chopped)
- 1 ½ cups of water
- 1 cup of scallions (sliced)
- 1 cup of fresh carrots (shredded)
- ½ cup of red wine vinegar
- 2 tbsp of sesame oil
- 2 tsp of green tabasco
- 2 tbsp of fresh garlic (chopped)
- 1 tbsp of ginger (chopped)
- 1 tbsp of soy sauce
- ¼ cup of fresh lime juice
- zest of 1 lime
- 4 tsp of chicken base
- 4 tsp of balsamic vinegar
- 2 tsp of dark molasses
- ¼ tsp of ginger
- ¼ tsp of black pepper
- ¼ tsp of garlic powder

Directions:

1. Mix the spaghetti, cocktail shrimp, scallions, broccoli, carrots, and mushrooms in a large bowl. Set aside for later.

2. Blend the red wine vinegar, sesame oil, tabasco, garlic, ginger, soy sauce, lime juice and zest, chicken base, balsamic vinegar, dark molasses, ginger, black pepper, and garlic in a blender for 1 minute. The texture of the final product should be smooth.

3. Pour the dressing over the pasta mixture, and toss all of the ingredients together until it is well coated to serve.

Food-prep tip: Store the vegetable and shrimp noodle salad in a glass airtight container for up to 4 days. Prep it on Sunday night for lunch meals for the next week.

Chapter 3: Snacks

Zucchini Pecan Muffins

These zucchini pecan muffins give you two out of your five recommended fruit and vegetable servings for the day. They make for a moist, delicious, low-protein snack that can be enjoyed late morning or afternoon to keep your energy going for the day.

Time: 35 minutes

Serving Size: 12

Prep Time: 15 minutes

Cook Time: 20 minutes

Nutritional Info:

Calories: 227

Carbs: 25.6 g

Fat: 13 g

Protein: 2.9 g

Sodium: 212.2 mg

Potassium: 212.2 mg

Phosphorus: 173 mg

Ingredients:

- 1 egg
- 1 ½ cups of flour (all-purpose)
- 1 cup of zucchini (shredded)
- ½ cup of white sugar
- ½ cup of olive oil
- ½ fresh blueberries
- ½ cup of pecans (chopped)
- ¼ cup of brown sugar
- ¼ cup of milk
- 1 ½ tsp of vanilla extract
- 1 tsp of cinnamon
- 1 tsp of baking soda

Directions:

1. Preheat the oven to 350°F, and line 12 muffin cups with paper cups.

2. Combine the dry ingredients in a medium bowl, including the flour, brown sugar, white sugar, baking soda, cinnamon, and salt.

3. Once the dry ingredients are combined, mix together the milk, egg, vanilla extract, and olive oil in a separate bowl until you've reached a smooth consistency.

4. Stir the wet mixture into the dry flour mixture until you've reached a batter consistency.

5. Add the blueberries, shredded zucchini, and pecans to the batter. Fill the muffin cups 2/3 full.

6. Bake the muffins in the preheated oven for 20 to 25 minutes until cooked through. Test this by inserting a toothpick into the muffin, and checking if it comes out clean.

Tortilla Chips and Dip

This snack is nice for when you are looking for something crispy to nibble on before lunch or dinner. It is very low in sodium, protein, fat, potassium, and phosphorus, which means that it ticks all the right boxes to support your kidney condition.

Time: 30 minutes

Serving Size: 4

Prep Time: 20 minutes

Cook Time: 10 minutes

Nutritional Info:

Calories: 56

Carbs: 10 g

Fat: 1 g

Protein: 2 g

Sodium: 81 mg

Potassium: 74 mg

Phosphorus: 48 mg

Ingredients:

- 2 cups of chopped fresh pineapple
- 2 8" whole-wheat tortillas (cut into wedges, rounds, or strips)
- ½ cup of red sweet pepper (finely chopped)
- 1 green onion (sliced)
- 1 tbsp of fresh cilantro (finely chopped)

Directions:

1. Preheat the oven to 375°F.

2. Arrange the tortilla wedges in a single layer onto a large baking sheet, and coat it lightly with cooking spray.

3. Bake the tortilla wedges for 10 minutes until they are golden brown and crisp. Once done, set them aside to cool down, then store them in a sealed container. The wedges should be stored at room temperature and should be consumed within 3 days.

4. Stir together the pineapple, sweet pepper, lime juice, green onion, and cilantro in a medium bowl, and cover it to chill for 24 to 48 hours.

5. Serve the tortilla wedges with a low-sodium dip of your choice, with a side of the fruit and vegetable mix.

Food-prep tip: Seal the tortilla chips in a Ziploc bag for up to 3 days. Enjoy it with a fresh, low-sodium dip in moderation.

Sweet and Savory Popcorn

With only 2 g of protein per serving, this sweet and savory snack is ideal for a variety of kidney conditions. It is gluten-free, and can be served seasoned or unseasoned.

Time: 5 minutes

Serving Size: 2 cups

Prep Time: 0 minutes

Cook Time: 5 minutes

Nutritional Info:

Calories: 120

Carbs: 12 g

Fat: 7 g

Protein: 2 g

Sodium: 2 mg

Potassium: 56 mg

Phosphorus: 60 mg

Ingredients:

- 8 cups of popcorn (air-popped)
- 2 tbsp of butter (unsalted)
- 2 tbsp of brown sugar
- ½ tsp of cinnamon
- ¼ tsp of nutmeg

Directions:

1. Heat the butter, cinnamon, brown sugar, and nutmeg over medium heat in a saucepan until the sugar melts and dissolves. Alternatively, the ingredients can be microwaved but should be monitored so that the butter doesn't burn.

2. Drizzle the spiced butter mixture over the popped popcorn. Mix the ingredients well before serving.

Food-prep tip: Preserve the coated popcorn in Ziploc bags for individual on-the-go servings. Store them a room temperature for up to 5 days.

Pumpkin Spice Yogurt

Whether it's Halloween or not, you get to enjoy spiced yogurt for a snack at any time of the year. Not only is this snack low in calories, but it can give you your calcium fix, boost your immune system, and make you feel like you're having dessert when you're sticking to a healthy, balanced diet. If you're not the meal-prep type, this snack is especially for you as it can be prepared in under five minutes.

Time: 3 minutes

Serving Size: 1

Prep Time: 3 minutes

Cook Time: 0 minutes

Nutritional Info:

Calories: 149

Carbs: 8 g

Fat: 4.2 g

Protein: 20 g

Sodium: 65.6 mg

Potassium: 35.75 mg

Phosphorus: 24.6 mg

Ingredients:

- 7 oz of plain Greek yogurt
- 1 tbsp of pumpkin puree
- ¼ tsp of cinnamon

- ¼ tsp of nutmeg
- ¼ tsp of honey

Directions:

1. Place the ingredients in a bowl and stir them together until they are well combined.

2. Serve the yogurt immediately, or store it in the refrigerator in an airtight container.

Food-prep tip: Make two to five servings more and store them in individual containers to take with you on the go. Keep the yogurt in the refrigerator for up to 5 days for a daily snack when you're tight on time.

Rosemary Roasted Almonds

As a source of healthy fats and Omega-3s, and serving as a savory snack, these roasted almonds are ideal for keeping you fuller for longer to prevent overeating and support weight loss. It can be prepped for a snack for the entire week and is quick and easy to make for a good source of protein appropriate for those with reduced kidney function.

Time: 25 minutes

Serving Size: 8

Prep Time: 5 minutes

Cook Time: 20 minutes

Nutritional Info:

Calories: 355

Carbs: 13 g

Fat: 31 g

Protein: 13 g

Sodium:223 mg

Potassium: 451 mg

Phosphorus: 298 mg

Ingredients:

- 2 cups of almonds (whole)
- 1 tbsp of olive oil
- 1 tbsp of rosemary (fresh, finely chopped)
- 1 sp of chili powder
- ¾ tsp of Himalayan salt
- ¼ tsp of cayenne pepper

Directions:

1. Preheat the oven to 325°F.

2. Combine the almonds, olive oil, rosemary, chili powder, Himalayan salt, and cayenne pepper in a small bowl.

3. Stir the ingredients well to coat the almonds.

4. Line a baking sheet with parchment paper and arrange the almonds with space between each. Bake them for 20 minutes before removing them from the oven.

Food-prep tip: Once cooled down, store the almonds in a Ziploc bag or sealed plastic container at room temperature or in the refrigerator for up to 5 days.

Berry Smoothie

For a delicious ice-cold smoothie, blend a variety of berries, including raspberries, blueberries, strawberries, and blackberries, to get an antioxidant and immune boost. This smoothie is low in calories, carbs, fat, and contains a good source of protein. It is also very low in sodium to support kidney function.

Time: 2 minutes

Serving Size: 2 (7 oz per serving)

Prep Time: 2 minutes

Cook Time: 0 minutes

Nutritional Info:

Calories: 152

Carbs: 15 g

Fat: 4 g

Protein: 14 g

Sodium: 84 mg

Potassium: 216 mg

Phosphorus: 76 mg

Ingredients:

- 4 oz of water (cold)
- 1 cup of frozen mixed berries
- ½ cup of coconut cream
- 1 tsp of berry maca powder
- 2 scoops of whey protein

Directions:

1. Add the frozen berries, water, and maca powder to the blender, and blend the ingredients at medium speed until they are mixed well.

2. Add coconut cream to the blender and blend to reach a creamy consistency.

3. Add protein powder to the smoothie and blend well.

4. Divide the smoothie into 2 servings, and serve the smoothies chilled right away.

Food-prep tip: Freeze the smoothie in a sealed container for up to 3 days to serve later.

Pumpkin Bread

Sometimes, all you may be craving is a tasty slice of bread. Although bread is limited on the kidney-friendly renal diet, nobody said anything about restricting pumpkin bread!

Time: 1 hour and 20 minutes

Serving Size: 10 (1 slice ¾" thick)

Prep Time: 10 minutes

Cook Time: 70 minutes

Nutritional Info:

Calories: 187

Carbs: 31 g

Fat: 6 g

Protein: 2 g

Sodium: 45 mg

Potassium: 69 mg

Phosphorus: 75 mg

Ingredients:

- 1 eggs
- 1 ¼ cups of flour (all-purpose)
- 1 cups of brown sugar
- ½ can of pumpkin (15 oz)
- ½ cup of whole cranberries (fresh)
- ¼ cup of vegetable oil

- 1 tsp of pumpkin pie spice

- 1 tsp of baking powder

Directions:

1. Preheat the oven to 350°F.

2. In a large bowl, combine the pumpkin pie spice, flour, and baking powder, and mix the dry ingredients well.

3. Add the eggs, pumpkin puree, brown sugar, and vegetable oil to a small mixing bowl, and beat the ingredients until properly blended.

4. Add the pumpkin mixture to the flour mixture, and stir everything until moistened. Continue to beat the mixture with a spoon until you've reached a good consistency without clumps.

5. Spoon the batter into a 9" x 5" loaf pan and bake the bread in the oven for 60 minutes.

6. Remove the pan from the oven, allowing them to cool for 10 minutes before slicing the bread into 10 ¾ inch-thick slices.

Food-prep tip: Store the pumpkin bread (sliced) in an airtight container in the refrigerator for up to 4 days.

Peanut Butter Bars

A little goes a long way. For a sweet and satisfying snack — 10 of them, to be exact — opt for this low-protein and low-carb treat, which contains a low source of sodium, potassium, and phosphorus to support your kidney health. This snack is vegetarian, gluten-free, and heart-healthy.

Time: 70 minutes

Serving Size: 10 (1 bar each)

Prep Time: 10 minutes

Cook Time: 60 minutes

Nutritional Info:

Calories: 275

Carbs: 26 g

Fat: 9 g

Protein: 8 g

Sodium: 102 mg

Potassium: 173 mg

Phosphorus: 120 mg

Ingredients:

- 2 cups of rolled oats
- ½ cup of whey protein powder
- ½ cup of peanut butter (melted)
- ¼ cup of mini dark chocolate chips

- ⅓ cup of honey
- ½ tsp of cinnamon
- ⅛ tsp of Himalayan salt (fine)

Directions:

1. Line a 5" x 8" baking dish with parchment paper.

2. Add the oats, cinnamon, and Himalayan salt to a medium bowl, and mix well.

3. Combine the protein powder, honey, and peanut butter in a medium bowl.

4. Add the wet mixture to the dry mixture, and mix everything until you have a well-blended sticky mixture.

5. Pat the mixture evenly into the lined baking dish, and sprinkle the top with dark chocolate chips. Pat the top of the dish to ensure there is an even layer on top.

6. Refrigerate the mixture for one hour.

7. Once done, remove the mixture from the refrigerator, and cut it into 5 sections. Half the 5 sections into 10 bars in total.

Food-prep tip: Wrap each bar in parchment paper or plastic wrap. Keep them refrigerated until for an on-the-go snack.

Roasted Garbanzo Beans

Roasted chickpeas, otherwise known as garbanzo beans, are terrific as a low-protein daily snack, and can also be enjoyed among friends as a light snack before a meal. They can be eaten plain, tossed up with a green salad, added to your favorite trail mix, and packed seasoned in your snack box for a busy day.

Time: 40 minutes

Serving Size: 4

Prep Time: 5 minutes

Cook Time: 35 minutes

Nutritional Info:

Calories: 96

Carbs: 15 g

Fat: 2 g

Protein: 6 g

Sodium: 369 mg

Potassium: 72.5 mg

Phosphorus: 48 mg

Ingredients:

- 15 oz of chickpeas/garbanzo beans (canned)
- 2 tsp of olive oil
- 1 tsp of garlic powder
- ⅛ tsp of kosher salt

Directions:

1. Preheat the oven to 375°F.

2. Drain and rinse the chickpeas, then pat dry them with a paper towel.

3. Arrange the chickpeas on a baking sheet and roast them for 30 minutes, removing the sheet from the oven every ten minutes to give them a good shake. The final product should be crunchy and golden brown, not moist. The chickpeas should be monitored closely to ensure they don't burn.

4. Combine salt and garlic powder in a medium bowl.

5. Remove the chickpeas from the oven once done, and add the olive oil over them immediately. Follow this by tossing the seasoning over them, and shaking them once more.

6. Allow them to cool before serving.

Food-prep tip: Store the chickpeas at room temperature in a Ziploc bag for up to 3 days. Prepare more in advance for snacks for busy weekdays.

Savory Roll Bites

These tasty bites offer a good source of protein and are a great alternative to the traditional sweet-treat protein balls. With a variety of flavors, it's an exciting snack you can look forward to every day.

Time: 10 minutes

Serving Size: 5 (2 balls per serving)

Prep Time: 10 minutes

Cook Time: 0 minutes

Nutritional Info:

Calories: 310

Carbs: 18.2 g

Fat: 16.8 g

Protein: 14 g

Sodium: 388 mg

Potassium: 205 mg

Phosphorus: 143 mg

Ingredients:

Pizza balls:

- ½ cup of white beans (drained and rinsed)
- ½ cup of almonds
- 2 tbsp of oat flour
- 1 tbsp of tomato paste
- 1 tbsp of nutritional yeast

- ½ tsp of Italian seasoning
- ⅛ tsp of kosher salt

Curry balls:

- ½ cup of white beans (drained and rinsed)
- ½ cup of cashews
- 2 tbsp of oat flour
- ½ tsp of garlic powder
- ½ tsp of curry powder
- ⅛ tsp of kosher salt

Garlic & herb balls:

- ½ cup of white beans (drained and rinsed)
- ¼ cup of tahini
- ¼ cup of oat flour
- ½ tsp of garlic powder
- ½ tsp of Italian seasoning
- ⅛ tsp of kosher salt

Directions:

1. Assemble three different types of balls by combining each set of ingredients separately in the food processor at a high speed. Pulse the ingredients until everything is well-combined. Do this starting with the pizza balls, followed by the curry balls, and then the garlic & herb balls. Clean the food processor each time after

you've blended one type and removed the contents.

2. Wet your fingers a little to prevent the dough from sticking. Use a ½ tbsp measure and scoop out some dough, and then roll it into spheres to create between 10 to 12 balls.

3. Store the savory bites in an airtight container and place them in the refrigerator for up to a week. They can also be frozen for up to 6 weeks.

Food-prep tip: Store the savory bites in individual containers or Ziploc bags to take them on the go during a busy week.

Chapter 4: Dinner

Chicken Noodle Soup

Who doesn't like chicken noodle soup on a cold winter's day, or even any other day when you feel like your immune system needs a boost of goodness? This recipe offers a light dinner option that is low in carbs and calories, a high-quality source of protein, and low mineral contents of sodium, potassium, and phosphorus. It also supports weight loss, diabetes, and is heart-healthy.

Time: 40 minutes

Serving Size: 10 servings (1 ¼ cups per serving)

Prep Time: 15 minutes

Cook Time: 25 minutes

Nutritional Info:

Calories: 185

Carbs: 14 g

Fat: 5 g

Protein: 21 g

Sodium: 361 mg

Potassium: 294 mg

Phosphorus: 161 mg

- 6 oz of noodles (uncooked)
- 8 cups of chicken broth (low-sodium)
- 4 cups of cooked chicken (cubed)
- 1 cup of carrots (diced)
- 1 cup of celery (diced)
- ½ cup of onion (diced)
- 3 tbsp of parsley (fresh)

Directions:

1. Bring the chicken broth to a boil in a large stockpot.

2. Add the diced vegetables, cubed chicken, and noodles to the pot.

3. Allow the soup ingredients to boil for at least 15 minutes until the noodles are properly cooked.

4. Garnish the soup with fresh parsley and serve it hot.

Food-prep tip: Store the chicken noodle soup in an airtight container in the refrigerator for up to 5 days, or freeze it for up to a month.

Vegetable Roast

This roast vegetable dish can be enjoyed on its own as a vegetarian meal, or with a lean source of protein like chicken breasts or white fish.

Time: 40 minutes

Serving Size: 6 servings (⅔ cup each)

Prep Time: 10 minutes

Cook Time: 30 minutes

Nutritional Info:

Calories: 141

Carbs: 14 g

Fat: 9 g

Protein: 2 g

Sodium: 7 mg

Potassium: 240 mg

Phosphorus: 48 mg

Ingredients:

- 2 cups of red potatoes (chopped into 1-inch cubes)
- ½ medium yellow bell pepper (diced)
- ½ medium red bell pepper (diced)
- 1 cup of button mushrooms (halved)
- ½ cup of zucchini (sliced)
- ¼ cup of olive oil

- 1 tbsp of garlic (minced)

- 2 tsp of rosemary (dried)

- 2 tsp of balsamic vinegar

- ½ tsp of black pepper

Directions:

1. Place the potatoes in a large pot of water on a stove over high heat, to boil for at least 10 minutes. Once done, drain the water and cook the potatoes until they are tender.

2. Mix together all of the vegetable ingredients in a medium bowl, except for the potatoes.

3. Spread the vegetables out on a sheet pan and sprinkle them with black pepper. Allow them to roast for 15 minutes until the vegetables are slightly browned. Stir them a few times while cooking.

4. Add the potatoes and the vegetables to a large bowl and toss with the balsamic vinegar. Serve them hot.

Food-pep tip: Store the roasted vegetables in an airtight container in the refrigerator for up to 3 days. Add a source of high-quality protein, like chicken breasts or white fish, to build a complete meal.

Lettuce Wraps

For a heart-healthy and diet-friendly meal that is both satisfying and scrumptious to eat, these lettuce wraps are filled with good flavor — minus the carbs. Chicken breasts can be pre-cooked over the weekend and shredded in advance for this meal.

Time: 30 minutes

Serving Size: 4 (2 wraps each)

Prep Time: 15 minutes

Cook Time: 15 minutes

Nutritional Info:

Calories: 219

Carbs: 4 g

Fat: 15 g

Protein: 17 g

Sodium: 103 mg

Potassium: 225 mg

Phosphorus:130 mg

Ingredients:

- 8 oz of chicken breast (cooked, shredded)
- 8 large lettuce leaves
- 2 scallions (sliced)
- ¼ cup of red onion (diced)
- ¼ cup of button mushrooms (halved)

- ¼ cup of cilantro

- 2 tbsp of rice vinegar (unseasoned)

- 2 tbsp olive oil

- 1 tbsp sesame oil

- 2 tsp of soy sauce (low-sodium)

- 2 tsp of garlic (minced)

Directions:

1. Mix the shredded chicken in a bowl with the garlic. Toss the ingredients to combine well.

2. Sauté the mixture in a medium non-stick pan with scallions, garlic, sesame oil, olive oil, rice vinegar, and soy sauce. Cook over medium heat for 15 minutes, and stir the ingredients several times to prevent them from burning.

3. Remove the chicken and place it in a serving bowl. Place ¼ cup of chicken in each of the lettuce leaves. Add 1 to 2 tsp of onion, red bell pepper, mushrooms, cilantro, and parsley on top. Wrap the lettuce around the mixture and serve.

Food-prep tip: Store the lettuce cups in an airtight container in the refrigerator for up to 2 days. Alternatively, store the ingredients individually and arrange the lettuce cups when serving them.

Garlic Shrimp Pasta

This pasta dish is delicious enough to leave you feeling like you've just had a cheat meal. However, the greatest thing of all is, you haven't. It's quick and easy to make and can serve an entire family.

Time: 20 minutes

Serving Size: 4 (1¼ cups each)

Prep Time: 5 minutes

Cook Time: 15 minutes

Nutritional Info:

Calories: 468

Carbs: 28 g

Fat: 28 g

Protein: 27 g

Sodium: 374 mg

Potassium: 469 mg

Phosphorus: 335 mg

Ingredients:

- 10 oz of cream cheese
- 4 oz of fettuccine (uncooked)
- ¾ oz of shrimp
- 1 ¾ cups of broccoli florets
- ¼ cup of red bell pepper (diced)
- ¼ cup of creamer
- ¼ cup of lemon juice
- 1 garlic clove (minced)
- ½ tsp of garlic powder
- ¾ tsp of black pepper

Directions:

1. Fill a medium pot three-quarters full with water and bring to a boil over high heat. Once the water is boiling, add the fettuccine pasta to the pot. Allow it to cook for 8 to 10 minutes, adding the broccoli for the final 3 minutes before removing it from the heat, draining the pasta, and setting it aside. Close the pot with a lid to lock in the heat.

2. Cook the shrimp and garlic over medium heat for 3 minutes in a non-stick pan, stirring often, until the shrimp is properly heated through.

3. Add the cream cheese, lemon juice, garlic powder, and black pepper. Cook the ingredients for 2 minutes.

4. Add the shrimp mixture to the pasta mixture, and stir to combine everything well.

5. Add a dash of black pepper to finish off the meal, and serve it hot.

Food-prep tip: Store the pasta dish in an airtight container in the refrigerator for up to 3 days.

Meat, Beans, and Corn Chili

This meat, beans, and corn chili is delectable, and surprisingly low in calories, too. It contains an excellent source of protein and is perfect if you are tight on time and looking to prepare a hot dish for a cold winter day. If this meal doesn't feel like comfort in a bowl, then what does! Additionally, it can be enjoyed with a nice crisp piece of ciabatta bread.

Time: 25 minutes

Serving Size: 8

Prep Time: 2 minutes

Cook Time: 23 minutes

Nutritional Info:

Calories: 217

Carbs: 18.7 g

Fat: 8.7 g

Protein: 17.5 g

Sodium: 268 mg

Potassium: 252 mg

Phosphorus: 168 mg

Ingredients:

- 15 oz of kidney beans
- 14.5 oz of roasted tomatoes (diced)
- 1 oz of beef (ground)
- 1 oz of turkey (ground)

- 2 cups of chicken stock
- 1 onion (diced)
- 3 tbsp tamari (gluten-free)
- 1 tbsp of avocado oil
- 1 tbsp of molasses
- 1 tbsp of kosher salt
- ½ tbsp of tomato paste
- 2 tsp of onion powder
- 2 cups of sweet corn (frozen)
- 1 ½ tsp of paprika
- 1 tsp of apple cider vinegar
- 1 tsp of cumin
- 1 tsp of garlic powder

Directions:

1. Heat the oil in a large stockpot over medium heat and cook the onion for around 5 minutes, until it is golden brown.

2. Add the ground beef and turkey and cook the meat until it is cooked through. Using the spatula, break everything into small pieces.

3. Add the kidney beans, roasted tomatoes, chicken stock, tamari, avocado oil, molasses, salt, tomato paste, onion powder, sweet corn, paprika, apple cider vinegar, cumin, and garlic powder to the pot's contents, and mix everything to combine well. Bring to a boil and

reduce the heat for it to simmer. Cover the pot and let simmer for up to 15 minutes.

4. Switch off the heat, and add black pepper to serve.

Food-prep tip: Store the chili in an airtight glass container in the refrigerator for up to 5 days.

Chicken Veggie Stir-Fry

For an Asian-inspired stir-fry dish, prepare this once a week for two people to keep for up to 3 days. This dish is low in calories and offers a quick and easy dinner that you can make within 30 minutes.

Time: 25 minutes

Serving Size: 6

Prep Time: 5 minutes

Cook Time: 10 minutes

Nutritional Info:

Calories: 279

Carbs: 38 g

Fat: 6 g

Protein: 17 g

Sodium: 196 mg

Potassium: 349 mg

Phosphorus: 180 mg

Ingredients:

- 12 oz of chicken breast (boneless and skinless)
- 3 cups of mixed vegetables (frozen)
- 3 cups of rice (cooked)
- 3 tbsp of honey
- 3 tbsp of pineapple juice
- 3 tbsp of vinegar
- 2 tbsp of olive oil

- 1 ½ tbsp of soy sauce (low-sodium)
- 1 ½ tbsp of cornstarch

Directions:

1. Rinse the chicken breasts and pat them dry before cutting them into 1-inch pieces. Set aside for later.

2. For the sauce, combine the vinegar, pineapple juice, honey, cornstarch, and soy sauce. Set the sauce aside.

3. Pour the olive oil into a large non-stick pan, and add more oil to cook the frozen vegetables in the pan for 3 to 5 minutes. Remove the vegetables from the heat once they are crisp and tender.

4. Add the chicken to the hot non-stick pan and stir-fry it for 4 minutes, or until fully cooked. Remove the chicken from the center of the pan, and stir in the sauce set aside earlier. Cook and stir the pan contents until the sauce is thick and makes bubbles.

5. Add the cooked vegetables back to the pan, and the ingredients together until everything is well coated. Continue cooking, stirring the contents, for 1 more minute.

6. Serve the stir-fry over a portion of rice.

Food-prep tip: Store the stir-fry and rice in separate sealed, airtight containers in the refrigerator for up to 3 days. Heat it up for an easy dinner after a long day at work.

Coconut Bean Curry

This curry dinner is infused with incredible flavors and is quick and easy to make to serve two people.

Time: 15 minutes

Serving Size: 2

Prep Time: 5 minutes

Cook Time: 10 minutes

Nutrition Info:

Calories: 418

Carbs: 34.4 g

Fat: 29 g

Protein: 10.6 g

Sodium: 469 mg

Potassium: 600 mg

Phosphorus: 398 mg

Ingredients:

- 15 oz of crushed tomatoes (canned)
- 15 oz of kidney beans (canned, drained)
- 14 oz of coconut milk (canned)
- 2 garlic cloves (minced)
- 1 cup of brown rice (cooked)
- 1 white onion (diced)
- 2 tbsp of vegetable oil (30 ml)

- 2 tbsp of ginger (grated)

- 1 tbsp of masala

- 1 tsp of soy sauce

- 1 tsp of fresh cilantro

- ½ tsp of lime juice

Directions:

1. In a large pot, heat the oil over medium to high heat and add the onion, ginger, garlic, and masala to the pot. Cook until the onion softens, which should be 4 to 5 minutes.

2. Add crushed tomatoes, kidney beans, coconut milk, and soy sauce to the pot, and allow it to simmer. Cook the contents for 10 minutes for the flavors to blend properly. Taste-test the curry and add more salt to increase the flavors.

3. Heat up the brown rice, then top with curry, fresh cilantro, and a drizzle of lime juice.

Food-prep tip: Store the bean curry and rice in separate airtight containers in the refrigerator for up to 4 days.

Crusted Steak Pie

This pot pie is a classic and traditional meal that can be enjoyed among family on its own or with a side of roasted vegetables.

Time: 1 hour and 40 minutes

Serving Size: 6

Prep Time: 10 minutes

Cook Time: 90 minutes

Nutritional Info:

Calories: 488

Carbs: 50.6 g

Fat: 18.2 g

Protein: 9.9 g

Sodium: 345 mg

Potassium: 288 mg

Phosphorus: 195 mg

Ingredients:

- 9" pastry (for the pie's crust)
- 2 lbs of steak (cubed)
- 2 onions (diced)
- 1 bay leaf
- 4 cups of potatoes (diced)
- 2 cups of water
- 6 tbsp of flour (all-purpose)
- 2 tbsp of lard
- 2 tsp of Worcestershire sauce
- 2 tsp of kosher salt
- ½ tsp of thyme (dried)
- ¼ tsp of black pepper

Directions:

1. In a large stew pot, add in the steak with the lard, followed by the onion, bay leaf, Worcestershire sauce, kosher salt, thyme, and black pepper. Then, add 1 ½ cups of water, bring to a boil, and allow it to simmer for an hour until the meat and vegetables are tender.

2. Add in the potatoes, and continue to simmer the pot contents until the potatoes are tender, which should take about 30 minutes.

3. Combine the flour and the remaining ½ cup of water. Stir it into the mixture, and continue stirring and cooking until the mixture thickens. Once done, pour it into a large pie dish.

4. Roll out the pastry so that it is bigger than the size of the casserole dish, and place it over the mixture. Trim the dough that hangs over the dish and fold it to seal. Cut a few steam vents in the center of the pie.

5. Bake the steak pie at 425°F for up to 30 minutes or until it is lightly browned. Serve hot.

Food-prep tip: Store the pie in an airtight container in the refrigerator for up to 3 days.

Crispy Salsa Tacos

Prepare these Mexican-inspired salsa tacos for a spicy and tasty dinner. It is a gluten-free, vegan option.

Time: 30 minutes

Serving Size: 8

Prep Time: 10 minutes

Cook Time: 20 minutes

Nutritional Info:

Calories: 130

Carbs: 20 g

Fat: 4.6 g

Protein: 3.8 g

Sodium: 203 mg

Potassium: 143 mg

Phosphorus: 98.2 mg

Ingredients:

Tortillas:

- 8 white corn tortillas
- avocado oil
- sea salt

Beans:

- 2 cups of pinto beans (canned and drained)
- ¼ tsp of chili powder

- ¼ tsp of cumin
- sea salt
- black pepper

Salsa:

- ½ cup of diced tomato
- ¼ cup of diced pineapple
- ¼ cup of cilantro (chopped)
- 3 tbsp of jalapeños (diced) - optional
- 3 tbsp of red onion (diced)
- 1 tbsp of lime juice
- kosher salt
- black pepper

Toppings:

- avocado (sliced)
- lime juice
- cilantro (fresh and chopped)

Directions:

1. Preheat the oven to 425°F and prep two baking sheets with parchment paper.

2. Lightly brush the corn tortillas with oil on both sides and sprinkle with sea salt. Follow this by stacking the baking sheets and lifting one side. Place as many tortillas as you can onto the edge, and lower the top baking sheet. Then,

fold the tortillas over the top to form a shell shape with each.

3. Bake the tortillas for 10 to 20 minutes, until they start to turn crisp and light brown, before removing them from a medium heat to cool down.

4. While the tortillas bake, add the pinto beans to a pot and bring to a boil over medium heat, and then lower the heat to simmer the beans until you're ready to add them to the tortilla. Season the beans with cumin, sea salt, and black pepper.

5. Prepare the pineapple salsa by adding all of the remaining ingredients to a small bowl. Toss them to coat, and then taste-test to adjust the flavors as per your preference. Salt can be added for the balance of flavor, lime for acidity, and pineapple for added sweetness.

6. When the tacos are slightly cooked, fill them with pinto beans and the pineapple salsa dressing.

Food-prep tip: Wrap the taco shells in a sheet of parchment paper to seal in freshness for longer. Store them in the refrigerator for up to 3 days.

Moroccan Chicken and Couscous Salad

This chicken and couscous salad is light and quick to make. Containing high-quality protein, this recipe is diabetic-friendly and heart-healthy.

Time: 15 minutes

Serving Size: 6 (2 cups per serving)

Prep Time: 5 minutes

Cook Time: 10 minutes

Nutritional Info:

Calories: 332

Carbs: 51.2 g

Fat: 6.6 g

Protein: 19.6 g

Sodium: 498 mg

Potassium: 322 mg

Phosphorus: 201 mg

Ingredients:

- 2 cups of water + 2 tbsp of water
- 2 cups of chicken (cooked and shredded)
- 1 ½ cups of couscous (uncooked)
- ½ cup of raisins
- ½ cup of orange juice concentrate (undiluted and thawed)
- ⅓ cup of lemon juice

- 2 tbsp of olive oil

- 2 tbsp of cumin

- ½ tbsp of green onions

- ½ tsp of kosher salt

- ¼ tsp of black pepper

Directions:

1. Boil 2 cups of water over medium to high heat in a medium pan. Once boiling, gradually add and stir the couscous and raisins. When it is done cooking, cover it and allow it to stand for 5 minutes, then fluff it with a fork.

2. Combine the orange juice, lemon juice, olive oil, cumin, kosher salt, and black pepper, whisking them together.

3. Combine the couscous mixture with the juice mixture, chicken, and 2 tbsp of water in a bowl. Toss the ingredients to mix, and then garnish them with green onions. Serve hot.

Food-prep tip: Store the chicken and couscous in an airtight container. Keep it in the refrigerator for up to 3 days.

Chapter 5: Desserts

Frosted Chocolate Cake

This cake is decadent and moist without the use of oil. It is also refined-sugar-free, using honey as its only sweetening ingredient. This cake tastes like a cheat meal, but it's low in calories, which means that it's a cleaner and healthier option for dessert.

Time: 1 hour and 32 minutes

Serving Size: 10

Prep Time: 25 minutes

Cook Time: 27 minutes + 40 minutes cooling time

Nutritional Info:

Calories: 292

Carbs: 59 g

Fat: 3 g

Protein: 13 g

Sodium: 305 mg

Potassium: 355 mg

Phosphorus: 215 mg

Ingredients:

Cake:

- 3 eggs
- 2 cups of Greek yogurt
- 2 cups of whole-wheat flour
- 1 cup of maple syrup
- ½ cup of cacao powder
- 1 ½ tsp of baking powder
- 1 tsp of baking soda
- 1 tsp of vanilla extract

Frosting:

- 1 ½ cups of plain Greek yogurt
- ⅓ cup of cacao powder
- ⅓ cup of maple syrup
- ½ tsp of vanilla extract

Directions:

1. For this recipe, you will need 2 cake pans. Place them on 2 large pieces of parchment paper, and circle the pans with a pencil on the outer part of the pans. Use scissors to cut out

the shape, place it inside of the cake pan, and spray with cooking spray, including the sides of the pan. Set the cake pans aside for later.

2. Preheat the oven to 350°F.

3. Add the eggs and the cake's maple syrup to a large mixing bowl. Use an electric mixer to beat for 30 seconds. Once done, add in yogurt, baking powder, baking soda, and vanilla. Beat the ingredients with the mixer once more for 30 seconds.

4. Add in the cacao powder, and use a whisk to mix well. Add in the flour, and whisk the mixture once more until you've reached a smooth consistency, but don't overmix it.

5. Divide the batter into two servings for the cake pans, and place them on the bottom rack of the oven for 27 minutes. Once done, test the cakes with a toothpick to see if it is baked through.

6. In the meantime, prepare the frosting by adding the yogurt, cacao powder, maple syrup, and vanilla to a bowl. Whisk the ingredients well and refrigerate the frosting until the cakes are ready to be decorated.

7. Once the cakes are ready, remove them from the oven and allow them to cool first before spreading a ¼ cup of frosting on each.

8. Decorate the cake as you wish and get creative with renal diet-friendly ingredients, such as

berries or dark chocolate chips, keeping in mind that any additions will alter the nutritional information. Cut the cake into 10 slices to serve.

Food-prep tip: Store the chocolate cake in the refrigerator in an airtight container for 4 to 5 days. The cake can also be frozen for up to 3 months.

Berry Crumble Squares

These berry squares are inspired by apple crumble, but with berries. It's a low-protein dessert that is also low in calories, and can serve as an ideal treat for someone with a sweet tooth, but who is on a sugar and protein-restricted diet.

Time: 60 minutes

Serving Size: 20

Prep Time: 20 minutes

Cook Time: 40 minutes

Nutritional Info:

Calories: 212

Carbs: 29 g

Fat: 9 g

Protein: 2 g

Sodium: 113 mg

Potassium: 46 mg

Phosphorus: 32 mg

Ingredients:

Crust & topping:

- 1 egg
- zest of 1 small lemon (finely grated)
- 3 cups of flour (all-purpose)
- 1 cup of granulated sugar
- 1 cup of butter (unsalted and cubed)
- 1 tsp of baking powder

- ⅓ tsp of vanilla extract

Berry filling:

- juice of 1 small lemon
- 4 ½ cups fresh berries (chopped)
- ¼ cup of granulated sugar
- 4 tsp of cornstarch

Directions:

1. Using a hand mixer, combine granulated sugar, flour, baking powder, and salt. Add the butter, lemon zest, egg, and vanilla to the mixture. Beat the ingredients at a low speed until the butter is distributed evenly. The mixture should have a crumbly consistency.

2. Add slightly more than half of the mixture to the bottom of the prepped pan, and use the bottom part of a measuring cup to press the dough evenly into the pan.

3. For the filling, gently stir the ingredients until they are well incorporated.

4. Spread the dessert's filling over the crust, and crumble the remaining dough over the berries.

5. Bake the crumble bars for 40 minutes. The top part of the dessert should be light golden brown. Once done, transfer the pan to a rack to cool before cutting it into 20 squares.

Food-prep tip: To store, place the crumble squares in an airtight container in the refrigerator for up to a week.

Banana Peanut Butter Cupcakes

For a low-protein option, these banana peanut butter cupcakes are just the thing to keep you and your family going all week long. Packed with clean ingredients, this dessert is also filled with essential nutrients and offers a nice pick-me-up after a long day at school or work.

Time: 35 minutes

Serving Size: 12

Prep Time: 5 minutes

Cook Time: 30 minutes

Nutritional Info:

Calories: 462.1

Carbs: 43.8 g g

Fat: 29.1 g

Protein: 6.4 g

Sodium: 181.3 mg

Potassium: 248 mg

Phosphorus: 163.3 mg

Ingredients:

Cupcakes:

- 2 bananas (ripe)
- 1 egg
- 1 egg yolk

- 1 ¼ cups of flour (all-purpose)
- ¾ cup of sugar
- ½ cup of butter (unsalted)
- ½ cup of sour cream
- 1 ½ tsp of vanilla extract
- 1 ½ tsp of baking powder
- 1 ½ tsp of vanilla extract
- ½ tsp of baking soda
- ¼ tsp of salt

Frosting:

- 8 oz of cream cheese (packaged)
- 1 ½ cups of powdered sugar
- ½ cup of butter (unsalted)
- ½ cup of peanut butter (smooth)
- ¼ cup of roasted peanuts (chopped and lightly salted)

Directions:

1. Preheat the oven to 350°F and line a standard 12-cup muffin tin with paper liners.

2. Whisk together the flour, baking soda, baking powder, and salt in a medium bowl.

3. Mash the bananas with a fork in a separate medium bowl until they are smooth. Add the cupcake's vanilla extract and sour cream to the bananas.

4. Use the electric mixer to beat the egg, butter and sugar in a large bowl for 3 minutes. The consistency should be light and fluffy. Once done, add the egg yolk and beat until it is well blended. Add the flour mixture, and beat the contents of the once more.

5. Divide the batter evenly among the 12 muffin cups, filling each ¼ full.

6. Bake the cupcakes for 20 minutes. Once done, remove them from the rack and allow them to cool.

7. For the frosting, sift the powdered sugar into a bowl. Then, add in the cream cheese, peanut butter, and butter. Use the electric mixer to beat the mixture until you've reached a smooth consistency.

8. Spread the frosting evenly on top of each of the cupcakes, followed by a handful of chopped peanuts.

Food-prep tip: Store these banana peanut butter muffins in an airtight container in the refrigerator for up to 4 days.

Cream Cheese Pie

This cream cheese pie is just that, creamy! It is low in protein, sodium, potassium, and phosphorus, offering all of the goodness in a dessert minus the guilt.

Time: 40 minutes

Serving Size: 8

Prep Time: 5 minutes

Cook Time: 35 minutes

Nutritional Info:

Calories: 237

Carbs: 35 g

Fat: 9 g

Protein: 4 g

Sodium: 220 mg

Potassium: 162 mg

Phosphorus: 91 mg

Ingredients:

- 8 oz of cream cheese (low-fat)
- 1 9" graham cracker crust (prepped)
- 3 cups of whipped cream (low-sugar, to top)
- 1 ½ cup of raspberries (fresh)
- 1 cup of blueberries (fresh)
- ½ cup of red raspberry preserves (low-sugar)

Directions:

1. For the filling, beat the whipped cream cheese and raspberry preserves with an electric beater on a medium speed, until it reaches a smooth consistency.

2. Fold the whipped cream topping into the cream cheese mixture.

3. Spread the filling layer evenly over the graham cracker crust base, and allow it to chill for 30 minutes in the refrigerator.

4. Before serving the cream pie, arrange the fresh blueberries and raspberries on top.

5. Add a dollop of whipped cream for the topping of the pie.

Food-prep tip: Store the cream pie leftovers in the refrigerator for up to 5 days. Cover it with tin foil or plastic wrap to seal in the pie's freshness.

Conclusion

The renal diet cookbook might have initially sounded like a diet that could come across as restrictive, but looking at this cookbook now, it's clear this is not the case. Packed with recipes from different cultures offering weight-loss benefits, being fit for anyone suffering from diabetes, and protecting heart health, this cookbook incorporated tasty dishes that can set you back on track to walking the health journey of your life. Apart from these additional benefits, the cookbook focuses on poor kidney function, especially for anyone living with CKD-non dialysis, dialysis, or any other renal condition.

Lowering protein contents in the body to ensure the blood remains clean of toxins and bacteria, and reducing one's intake of sodium, potassium, and phosphorus, the renal diet cookbook takes care of all your needs — some of which may have seemed challenging to deal with before. By simplifying recipes and making them delicious, it won't even feel like you're bound by restrictions and rules while following your kidney-friendly diet.

References

Allison. (2018, July). *Berry Crumble Bars - Celebrating Sweets*. Celebrating Sweets. https://celebratingsweets.com/mixed-berry-crumble-bars/

American Kidney Fund. (2020, June 17). *Kidney-friendly diet for CKD*. Kidneyfund.org. https://www.kidneyfund.org/kidney-disease/chronic-kidney-disease-ckd/kidney-friendly-diet-for-ckd.html

Apple Cinnamon Maple Granola. (n.d.). *Www.davita.com. Retrieved March 27, 2021, from https://www.davita.com/diet-nutrition/recipes/breakfast-brunch/apple-cinnamon-maple-granola*

Banana Cupcakes with Peanut Butter Frosting. (2015, March 17). Epicurious. https://www.epicurious.com/recipes/food/views/banana-cupcakes-with-peanut-butter-frosting-358240

BBQ Chicken Pita Pizza. (n.d.). *Www.davita.com. Retrieved March 28, 2021, from https://www.davita.com/diet-nutrition/recipes/pizza-sandwiches/bbq-chicken-pita-pizza*

Blueberry Dream Muffins. (n.d.). Www.davita.com. Retrieved March 25, 2021, from https://www.davita.com/diet-nutrition/recipes/breads/blueberry-dream-muffins

Cheesesteak Quiche Recipe. (n.d.). Fresenius Kidney Care. Retrieved March 25, 2021, from https://www.freseniuskidneycare.com/eating-well/recipes/breakfasts/cheesesteak-quiche

Chicken Lettuce Wraps. (n.d.). *Www.davita.com. Retrieved March 29, 2021, from https://www.davita.com/diet-nutrition/recipes/pizza-sandwiches/chicken-lettuce-wraps*

Chilled Veggie and Shrimp Noodle Salad. (n.d.). Fresenius Kidney Care. Retrieved March 28, 2021, from https://www.freseniuskidneycare.com/eating-well/recipes/lunches/chilled-veggie-and-shrimp-noodle-salad

Crispy Baked Vegan Tacos | Minimalist Baker Recipes. (2016, May 5). Minimalist Baker. https://minimalistbaker.com/crispy-baked-tacos/

Croxton, Diana. (n.d.). *Easy Turkey Breakfast Burritos. Fresenius Kidney Care. Retrieved March 25, 2021, from https://www.freseniuskidneycare.com/eating-well/recipes/breakfasts/easy-turkey-breakfast-burritos*

DeHart, Adrienne. (n.d.) *Recipe: Crispy Chicken and Avocado Burrito Wraps.* (n.d.). SelectHealth.org. Retrieved March 28, 2021,

from
https://selecthealth.org/blog/2020/08/chicke
n-avocado-burrito-wraps

Easy Turkey Sloppy Joes. (n.d.). Www.davita.com.
Retrieved March 28, 2021, from
https://www.davita.com/diet-
nutrition/recipes/chicken-turkey/easy-turkey-
sloppy-joes

E. P. a loving, Children, M. of T. H., delicious, I. am
obsessed with teaching people how to make, &
gut! (2016, May 6). *Homemade Chili Recipe
with Kidney Beans.* Nurture My Gut.
https://nurturemygut.com/homemade-chili-
recipe-with-kidney-beans.html/

Ford, Mathea. (n.d.). *Breakfast for Chronic Kidney
Disease.* (2015, September 21). Renal Diet
Menu Headquarters.
https://www.renaldiethq.com/breakfast-for-
chronic-kidney-disease/

Glenda. (n.d.). *Steak and Kidney Pie II.* Allrecipes.
Retrieved March 29, 2021, from
https://www.allrecipes.com/recipe/12477/ste
ak-and-kidney-pie-ii/

Gutwald, Katie, RD. (2019, October 28). *Pumpkin
Spice Yogurt Recipe.* (n.d.).
Type2Diabetes.com. Retrieved March 29,
2021, from
https://type2diabetes.com/recipes/pumpkin-
spice-yogurt

Healthy Blueberry Cobbler. (2020, April 2). *Erin Lives Whole. https://www.erinlives whole.com/healthy-blueberry-cobbler/*

Holiday Morning French Toast. (n.d.). Www.davita.com. Retrieved March 27, 2021, from https://www.davita.com/diet-nutrition/recipes/breakfast-brunch/holiday-morning-french-toast

How to Make Roasted Chickpeas. (2019, July 24). Super Healthy Kids. https://www.superhealthykids.com/recipes/roasting-beans/

Images sourced from *Freepik - Free Graphic resources for everyone. (2019). Freepik.* https://www.freepik.com/

Images sourced from Pixabay. (2018). *Pixabay.* Pixabay.com. https://pixabay.com/

K, Sarah. (2015, August 9). https://www.diabetesdaily.com/blog/roasted-almonds-with-rosemary-95880/

Knock-Your-Socks-Off Chicken Broccoli Stromboli. (n.d.). Fresenius Kidney Care. https://www.freseniuskidneycare.com/eating-well/recipes/lunches/knock-your-socks-off-chicken-broccoli-strombol

Lawless, Laura, BASc. (2020, June 10). *Mediterranean Bean Salad.* The Recipe Well. https://therecipewell.com/mediterranean-bean-salad/

Levin, Karen, A. (2000, May). *North African Chicken and Couscous Recipe.* MyRecipes. https://www.myrecipes.com/recipe/north-african-chicken-couscous

Mexican Seasoning. (n.d.). *Www.davita.com. Retrieved March 28, 2021, from https://www.davita.com/diet-nutrition/recipes/sauces-seasonings/mexican-seasoning*

Mixed Berry Protein Smoothie. (n.d.). Www.davita.com. Retrieved March 29, 2021, from https://www.davita.com/diet-nutrition/recipes/beverages/mixed-berry-protein-smoothie

Mushroom & Red Pepper Omelet. (n.d.). *Www.davita.com. Retrieved March 27, 2021, from https://www.davita.com/diet-nutrition/recipes/breakfast-brunch/mushroom--red-pepper-omelet*

NephCure Kidney International ®. (2018). Nephcure.org. https://nephcure.org/livingwithkidneydisease/diet-and-nutrition/renal-diet/

No-Bake Peanutty Oat Bars. (n.d.). Www.davita.com. Retrieved March 29, 2021, from https://www.davita.com/diet-nutrition/recipes/breakfast-brunch/no-bake-peanutty-oat-bars

Olena. (2021, January 8). *Healthy Chocolate Cake {No Oil and So Moist}.* IFOODreal.com.

https://ifoodreal.com/healthy-chocolate-cake/

Omelet. (2019, June 17). *Omelet.* (2019, June 17). Blog RenalTracker. https://blog.renaltracker.com/low-potassium-recipe/omelet/?utm_source=pinterest&utm_medium=pin_post

Pumpkin Cranberry Bread. (n.d.). Www.davita.com. Retrieved March 29, 2021, from https://www.davita.com/diet-nutrition/recipes/breads/pumpkin-cranberry-bread

Rainbow Chips & Dip. (n.d.). *Parents. Retrieved March 29, 2021, from https://www.parents.com/recipe/appetizers-snacks/rainbow-chips-dip/*

Red, White and Blue Pie. (n.d.). Www.davita.com. Retrieved March 29, 2021, from https://www.davita.com/diet-nutrition/recipes/desserts/red-white-and-blue-pie

Roasted Rosemary Chicken and Vegetables. (n.d.). Www.davita.com. Retrieved March 28, 2021, from https://www.davita.com/diet-nutrition/recipes/chicken-turkey/roasted-rosemary-chicken-and-vegetables

Roasted Vegetable Salad. (n.d.). *Www.davita.com. Retrieved March 29, 2021, from https://www.davita.com/diet-*

nutrition/recipes/salads-dressings/roasted-vegetable-salad

Rotisserie Chicken Noodle Soup. (n.d.). Www.davita.com. Retrieved March 29, 2021, from https://www.davita.com/diet-nutrition/recipes/soups-stews/rotisserie-chicken-noodle-soup

Sarah. (2020, September 28). *Easy Coconut Kidney Bean Curry (Under 15 Minutes)*. (2020, June 12). Live Eat Learn. https://www.liveeatlearn.com/coconut-kidney-bean-curry/

3 Savory Energy Ball Recipes for On the Go Snacking. (2017, September 4). From My Bowl. https://frommybowl.com/savory-energy-ball-recipes/

Shoemaker, Caitlin. (2017, September 4). https://frommybowl.com/savory-energy-ball-recipes/

Shrimp Quesadilla. (n.d.). Www.davita.com. Retrieved March 28, 2021, from https://www.davita.com/diet-nutrition/recipes/seafood/shrimp-quesadilla

Speedy Chicken Stir-Fry. (n.d.). Www.davita.com. Retrieved March 29, 2021, from https://www.davita.com/diet-nutrition/recipes/chicken-turkey/speedy-chicken-stir-fry

Spicy Tofu Scrambler Recipe. (n.d.). Fresenius
    Kidney Care. Retrieved March 26, 2021, from
    https://www.freseniuskidneycare.com/eating-
    well/recipes/breakfasts/spicy-tofu-scrambler

Strawberry & Cream Cheese Sandwich. (2007,
    September). EatingWell. Retrieved March 28,
    2021, from
    https://www.eatingwell.com/recipe/249521/s
    trawberry-cream-cheese-sandwich/#nutrition

tastes, R. R. M. L. A. low potassium beverage for all, &
    says, occasions-Kidney R. (2017, February 3).
    *Blueberry Smoothie: A Simple Low Potassium
    Recipe!* Kidney RD.
    https://kidneyrd.com/low-potassium-
    blueberry-smoothie/

Printed in Great Britain
by Amazon

79489462R00079